And a voice cried out,
In the wilderness
Prepare a path for the Lord.

And a voice cried out in the wilderness,
This is my Son - in whom I am well pleased.

SPLINTERS

Mary Kennelly and Brenda Fitzmaurice

Evensong Publications

First Edition
Published by Evensong Publications
2017
Evensong Publications, Ballycullane, Glin, County Limerick,
Ireland
email: evensongpublications@gmail.com

ISBN   978-0-956 6687-1-4

Cover Illustration **Desert** (2015) by Brenda Fitzmaurice
Graphic design by Tom Moore, Janus Design, Glin, Co Limerick
Photography by Tom Moore and Trevor O'Donoghue
Printed by Walsh Colour Print, Castleisland, Co. Kerry

For Mary & Tom Moore
With deep gratitude for three decades of friendship
Love Mary

For all my Marys
Love Brenda

CONTENTS

FOREWORD

The poet Mary Kennelly and the painter Brenda Fitzmaurice achieve an almost perfect collaboration of poet and artist. Splinters, is the second book of poetry and image that they have worked on together. From the Stones, was published by Evensong Publications in 2010.

Mary and Brenda are lifelong friends who share a passion for poetry and painting. Both are assured artists. Kennelly's introspections are a deeply human, thought provoking retelling of stories from the Bible. Fitzmaurice's paintings evoke the silence and texture of both intimate and otherworldly space. Their individual, distinctive voices, (Kennelly's through the word, Fitzmaurice's through image) resonate with an understanding of the powerful literary and visual heritage that is the Judeo Christian Bible. These are stories that have relevance in contemporary society and confront us with aspects of human behaviors that are primordial. The poems awaken us to the importance of 'stories' as an authentic history of the ordinary, the often marginalized, those omitted from conventional history.

The poems have their roots in traditional story telling and the poet aligns herself firmly within that tradition but Kennelly takes a fresh look at the old tales. She gives peripheral characters a voice : Mother in Law, The Working Man, women gossiping in, In His Own Town. Her language is direct and clear, heartfelt but not didactic in tone. Her interpretations are inclusive and broad in the best sense.

Kennelly's aesthetic is grounded in the familial; she speaks out of an engagement and love of community and place. She reminds us that in the telling and retelling of stories we recognize ourselves and can perhaps understand and empathize more fully with humanity.

Fitzmaurice's paintings interpret meaning as beauty. Her wonderfully worked images are startling in their luminosity. Patterns of paint can change from a blaze of light to a sulky glow, often shot through with shafts of light. Dense shadows suggest emotional depth and her unique application of paint indicates an inherent anxiety of being. This artist intuits her interpretation of the subject matter and she has the confidence in her ability as a painter, to make manifest her individual expression. She translates these stories into paintings imbued with a particular simplicity and felt lushness.

Successful collaborations depend on the willingness of both to engage and appreciate each other's work, to allow each the space to develop their common themes. It seems to me that Mary and Brenda have the wisdom and generosity to do this. Splinters, is a beautiful book, it is a tribute to their enduring passion for poetry and painting and their friendship.

Jo Slade 2017

INTRODUCTION

Stories were a source of endless fascination to me as a child, as they are with all children.

In 1988 I went to St Patrick's College, Maynooth to commence studying for a Bachelor's degree in Theology and Arts and I fell in love with another story. In the study of scripture I had found a world that captured me, one that has held me ever since.

Like countless others throughout the world, I have returned time and again to the scriptures and in particular to the Gospel story. One area of interest for me has been the story of how the Gospel has been handed down – the redactions, the additions, the omissions, the translations and the interpretations. Like many others, I have wondered if it is possible to find the historical Jesus behind centuries of transmission. Who was this Jesus: Son of God or Christo-Roman invention? Many of the finest historians and theologians have grappled - and continue to grapple - with this question. So much has been written about the Jesus story that it is possible to argue that any further exploration is merely retracing what has already been uncovered.

Yet the story continues to pull in generation after generation and it exists because of the mesmerising character of a 1st century carpenter's son and his extraordinary impact on the lives of those who came into contact with him.

Why, after the seemingly abject failure of his mission through the ignominy of a criminal's death, did his followers not simply return home? Return to their families and communities, to their fields or their fish? What would prompt them to leave all comforts behind and to risk their lives in order to tell a story?

This collection is a mishmash of individual voices seeking to tell of their encounter with the carpenter's son. Each voice is just an imagined splinter: a tiny part of a greater whole that perhaps when seen together creates a recognisable story… or perhaps not. This collection is not intended to proselytise or evangelise. No offence is intended nor ownership implied.

For this collection the challenge was to take this mishmash of voices and to allow them to speak to me through snatches or words, and to Brenda Fitzmaurice through her own artistic vision. It was both fascinating and humbling to watch Brenda's work process and the way in which she was able to bring her vision to the collection.

I have loved working on these stories and sharing that journey with Brenda. Her talent and vision made the journey possible; her generosity and friendship made the journey enjoyable.

M. Kennelly

SPLINTERS   *Oil on Canvas   76cm x 60cm 2015*

SPLINTERS

Through frenzy, chaos, desire and distress
In the infinitesimal space
Between one shuddering breath
And the next,
I exhale.
Aeons of tears and of secrets and of songs
The poet whose voice is never heard
The weeping mother without her child
The rotting fools who thought their reign
Would never end
I exhale.
Transient splinters of sights and tastes and sounds
That for one tantalising second
In the cold mist of dawn
Come together to make story

FATHER SONG   *Oil on Canvas   40cm x 40cm 2017*

FATHER SONG

You are my son
The child that God
Saw fit to gift to me.
Your hand is weak
While mine is strong.
My life's blessing
Will be to show to you
What it takes to be a man.
My greatest gift will be
To love and comfort you,
To listen to your tales,
To hear of all your woes,
To gather all the smiles
That you have the time to share.
Your burdens will be mine
I will suffer all your pains.
I wish that I could learn to scrub
The world of every harm
That might ever think to visit you.
It humbles me to know
That I will have to learn
To one day let you go
As you strike out on your own.
I know I will be old and frail
Before my job is done
But I will never cease my task
Because you are my son.

SPRING

As the days grow longer
We have time –
When all the work
Young hands must do
Is finally done –
To throw a ball around.
Quick, keep it up
It must not touch the ground
If you are to win.
The world to come
Is nothing to us now.
There is just this moment
And this time
And our laughter
And our game
And you and me
Under the shade
Of the waiting olive tree.

SPRING

Oil on Canvas
40cm x 40cm 2015

APOSTLE   *Oil on Canvas   40cm x 40cm   2015*

APOSTLE

It wasn't when he called me first to him
As he waited confidently on silent shore.
It wasn't the fearful rightness of his words
Although they burnt straight through to my core.
Nor was it all the powerful things he did –
Feeding five thousand with scarcely fish or bread
Or how he overlooked my fiery temper and mistakes
With a smile and a laying on of hands upon my head.
It wasn't even when he told me I was his
To build his every hope upon
And that he would use that very bullishness
As the strength he would be starting from.
It was, instead, in my most painful moment
After I had shamed myself with lies
- Hating myself for my betrayal -
When I looked up and was captured by his eyes
I accepted there was never any going back
To the simple life I'd loved upon the sea.
His inexplicable forgiveness poured me out.
He finally made an apostle out of me.

ALCHEMY   *Oil on Canvas   40cm x 40cm 2016*

ALCHEMY

What does it matter if, from time to time,
I yearn for the 'me' I was before there was an 'us'?
I know the truth and the truth is that
Whatever comes, 'I' will make no return.
You told us that there would be no easy way
If we choose to follow down your path.
You promised fire and sword not peace.
But I wonder, if you fully understood
The irresistible alchemy of suffering
On a wooden cross or the pilgrims' road?
I am changed beyond all imagination now
I am not the same metal that I was before.
You came and knocked and called me out
And I, little knowing, opened the door.

SANDALS

They grabbed me and groped me
They shouted and spat
They dragged me undone through the streets
Then threw me for judgement
At his sandalled feet.
I shook from the terror - they did not care -
Head down from the weight of my shame
I struggled to cover my skin.
Rough, righteous men shouted my sin
And asked him what should be done?
With shuddering breaths
I waited for condemnation
My eyes on his feet –
Nothing out of the ordinary,
Not all that different from the man
Whose soft words led me to my crime.

"Let him without sin throw the first stone."
More soft words leading to hard stones,
Naked humiliation, then death.
Looking at his feet I waited
For the first sharp sting of pain
That somehow never came.
"Woman, has no one condemned you?
Then neither do I.
Go, but sin no more."
His hand under my trembling chin,
I looked into fathomless eyes.
What, I wondered, was I to do –
With this … forgiveness? –
But pull myself together
And follow in his sandalled feet.

SANDALS

Oil on Canvas
40cm x 40cm 2017

CANA   *Oil on Canvas   40cm x 40cm 2016*

CANA

A gift from my God - beyond all I had done -
This trembling beautiful bride
To be my comfort and my home
To be mother to my daughters and my sons.
I did not care that some would say
She did not bring her fair portion
To the business of our life.
In truth, I would have taken her
Without a penny to her name.
I knew there would be time enough
For us to find our path.
But first a wedding feast, a celebration
With our families and our friends.
Until the steward came and told
How the wine was almost gone
And in my beloved's trembling shame
I saw our joy in pieces at our feet
And wondered what could be done.
Then I saw Mary go and speak
Quiet words to her wandering son.
Moving as she always does,
Without any fuss.
Then there was wine
And my beloved's smile –
That, to me, was beyond miraculous.

HAEMORRHAGE *Oil on Canvas   40cm x 40cm 2017*

HAEMORRHAGE

While other women's wombs
Gave birth to life
From mine flowed only slaughter.
From the days I was a girl, the bleeding came
Leaching life and lustre in its trail.
While my younger sisters flourished
I became the cursed daughter.
No man would think to take me on
Thrown down so many days each month,
Until the day he saw me resting
From the midday sun beneath a shading tree
And then he promised in his gentle way
That he would make his life with me.
He tried, I know, to keep his word
But dead babies in their wake
Tear the strongest love apart.
When I saw the cooling in his eyes
My desperation drove me on
To seek the teacher out.
I saw him as he left his boat
I pushed to cross his path
But in the end I could not reach him
Thrown aside by others in the crowd.
I was incensed that once again
I was to be the one denied.
For that reason, I reached out
And I touched his passing cloak.

HUNGER PAINS

No chores today - we left early,
Wrapped against the morning breeze.
My mother and father smiling,
Swinging me as they walked.
Out from our village and up and up
Until we were surrounded by others -
So many others - travelling as well.
All day we listened to words
Passed along by the crowds.
As my father heard he called them out
Again and again and again
As he looked into my mother's eyes.
They did not notice the day go by
But I did for I was hungry.
I began, after a time, to cry
Big tears filled with my tragedy.
Then there was food -
Bread and fish -
I ate away at my will.
And I felt everything was right,
I was once again happy
As we walked home in dark.

HUNGER PAINS
Oil on Canvas
40cm x 40cm 2015

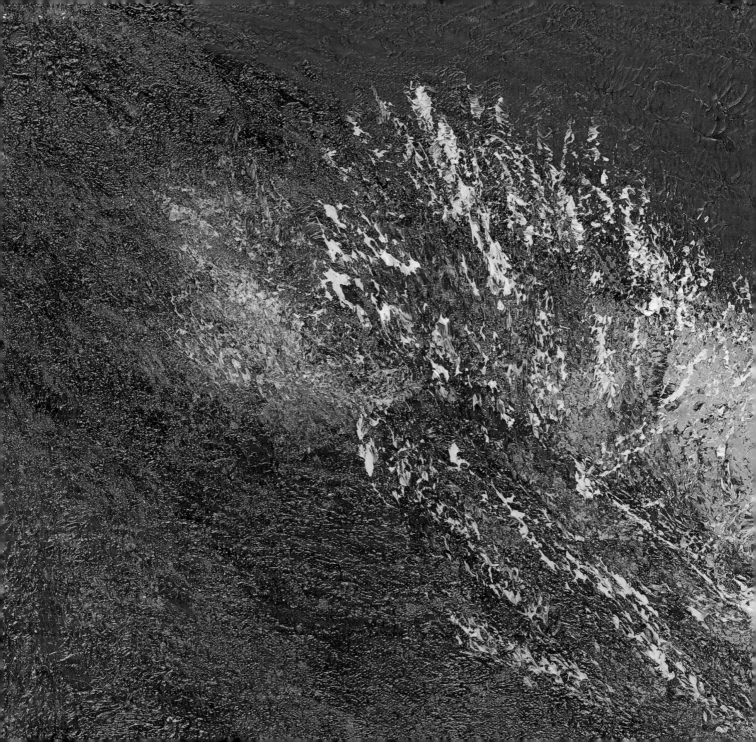

DEMONIAC

 It rose from inside me, a wild beast
Tearing through all my possibilities,
Frightening family and denying dignity
Casting me into the darkness
Beyond the reach of God and man
A white noise and a white foam
Until I was nothing but a spent force
Unable to rise from my spot on the floor.

Then there was him –
Surrounded by frenzy -
Standing silent in their midst
Promising not just a cure
But finally,
After years of pain, the fragrant hope
That I, miserable as I am,
Might be allowed some semblance of peace.

DEMONIAC
Oil on Canvas
30cm x 30cm 2016

TABLE FELLOWSHIP   *Oil on Canvas   25cm x 25cm 2015*

TABLE FELLOWSHIP

I do not know that he is all they think or say he is.
There was no magic in his time with me -
Unless you call it magic that he could see
Beyond the throng, into the dark place
Where I hid, reluctant to face
The all-pervasive judgement
Of those who set themselves
Above a little man like me.
Not magic, I think, but majesty
In the moment when he looked past
Those self-appointed puritans and said,
"Come, friend, I choose your household
To rest and wash and to break bread."

IN HIS OWN TOWN

Sure, wouldn't you have to feel sorry for her,
With her husband gone and that son of hers
Run wild all over the place?
They say he sits with common whores
While he eats bread with Roman collaborators
And surrounds himself with a hopeless crew
Of simpletons and layabouts.
And worst of all, this Sabbath past, he took to talking
In the synagogue, like he was some big man
And telling decent living folk what they were doing wrong!
He's lucky he escaped with his skin almost intact for sure.
But as I say, it's his mother that I feel sorry for.

IN HIS OWN TOWN
Oil on Canvas
40cm x 40cm 2017

ANOINTED

No-one understood.
I wept not for my sins
But for your pain.
They seemed to miss
The shadows in your eyes,
Or perhaps it was excitement
And the noise thick in the air
Took their attention
From the lines etched
Deeply in your face.
I saw. It made me cry.
I heard the undertones
Of a thing I could not bear
To even think about
Held fast within your voice.
I cleaned you with my tears
And dried you with my hair
And anointed you for slaughter,
In case there would be no time
To make such preparations after.

ANOINTED

Oil on Canvas
40cm x 40cm   2015

PILATE'S REPORT

Another day of ceaseless heat and endless dust
And sounds and smells that are not of my home.
Another gathering in praise of their defeated God
That sees them wash and pray and sing in desperation.
Another rebel promising that he would bring salvation –
Sending pragmatic priests scurrying to my courts
In feigned concern for Caesar and for Rome.
They cry out for his blood as if it was a sport.
Another chance for them to test their skills
In manipulating, for their ends, both Rome and I.
Another tree is put to use to demonstrate the ease
With which, I will let any number of their saviours die.

PILATE'S REPORT
Oil on Canvas
40cm x 40cm 2017

DENIAL

No sir, I do not know him, I tell you.
I thought I did but the man I knew
Was not the kind to draw down the heavens
On our helpless hearts and heads.
In search of what, I cannot say.
The man I knew was gentle in his ways
Like dawn flirting timidly with the night sky
Until his light won softly out
And every trace of dark was gone.

No sir, I do not know this man
Riding triumphant into this place
To glory and the singing of crowd song.
The man I followed was tender with his words,
Pouring them like balm on wounded hearts
Then leaving silence to bring his peace along.

In truth sir, I know nothing of this man
Who turns tables and the world upon itself
The man I loved brought healing with his hands.

DENIAL
Oil on Canvas
40cm x 40cm 2017

WHY HAVE YOU FORSAKEN ME?

Shivering
Shuddering
Struggling
Beaten
Bruised
Bleeding
Torn apart
Naked
And alone.
Weren't you supposed to stay with me?
"My God! My God, Why have you forsaken me?"

WHY HAVE YOU FORSAKEN ME?

Acrylic on Canvas
40cm x 40cm 2017

IT IS FINISHED

It is finished.
I am done.
I have scraped myself
Out for love of you.
I cannot say for sure
What was lost or won.
I know nothing now
Beyond this simple fact:
It is finished.
I am done.

IT IS FINISHED

Oil on Canvas
40cm x 40cm 2017

BODY AND BLOOD   *Oil on Canvas   40cm x 40cm   2016*

BODY AND BLOOD

Battered beyond recognition
They gave him back to me.
Too late to prepare him
As I would have done.
I wept at the kindness
Of the shadowed man
Even though I thought
I had no more tears to shed.
I took the long white cloth
A shroud –
Oh how can that be right? –
To cover body and blood.
And with the women who remained,
Picked flowers in lieu of oils.
We struggled to move him
There was no part of him not torn.
Body and blood
So much spilled blood
And a white shroud
In a dark cave.
All that was left of my love.

AFTER   *Oil on Canvas   40cm x 40cm 2015*

AFTER

This is a moment after.
Even if every morning clouds my brain
For tantalising, heart-breaking seconds
This is always just another moment after.
Sent, it seems, to teach me yet again
That some wounds cannot be healed.
A break is known by the space between and
All my tears and wishes cannot alter fact.
This is yet another of those moments
To be survived with gritted teeth and
There is no joy here to be found because
This is a moment after.
A moment after the fracture.

TOMB   *Oil on Canvas*   *40cm x 40cm*   *2016*

TOMB

In truth, it was not for any of the words he spoke
Though they had felt like eagles in my heart.
I had seen such fire before and was wise enough
Not to be consumed myself by flames
When it became inevitable that he would suffer
For turning words against powers he could not best.
Nor was it what they did to turn him from a man
Into a quivering sobbing bleeding mess.
It was the tragedy of our times that we witnessed
Such savagery on an almost daily basis.
Nor the fact that, in the end, all his brothers
Left him to die surrounded only by his women
Kneeling, weeping at his cross.
Fear makes cowards of most men.
It was her, when it was done and they took him down
And laid him at her breast- no polite keening then
But gutting guttural sounds torn from the fabric of the earth
That bade me finally step forward and say
Follow me and for your love of him come lay him in my tomb
You deserve more than to have his lacerated body thrown away.

THE TWIN   *Oil on Canvas   40cm x 40cm 2017*

THE TWIN

I am Didymos Judas Thomas, the twin.
From my very first stuttering breath
There was me and there was him.

Of course I followed where he led,
Through dust and fields and waters
Where he slept, there I lay my head.

It was me who saw behind his smile
As he grew silent and more fearful
While we travelled mile by mile.

I saw my worries reflected in his eyes
So I carried his worries in my heart –
His torment the reason for my silent cries.

Then he went where I could not go.
For a twin there can be nothing worse.
It was almost like a killing blow

To watch him from my hiding place.
I suffered through his every hurt
Then watched his life leave my own face.

When they said that he and I could further meet
My pain answered that I would not believe
Until I touched his desecrated hands and feet.

LOSS

When did I lose him?
When was it too late?
On that hateful tree?
When he came to power hungry Jerusalem
And left his chairs behind in Galilee?
Or was it when they followed him
And listened to his every word?
Or when he fell hopelessly in love with God?

When did I lose him?
When was it too late?
My arms are empty and numb
For the sake of the world
Do you think I can accept what has been done?
What do I care for a kingdom yet to come?
Oh God, I am a mother first
What good is a redeemed world to me
At the cost of a beautiful son?

LOSS
Oil on Canvas
40cm x 40cm 2016

CENTURION

A small strange land
With a small strange people
And their beloved small strange God.
Troublesome all
More than their worth.
But there was that one man
With eyes that were aged
And seemed to know all.
He made me believe
He could save just by his will.
Of course - like the rest of his land
Even he fell afoul of the law.
They say he met a bad end.

CENTURION

Oil on Canvas
40cm x 40cm   2016

CAIAPHAS   *Oil on Canvas*   *40cm x 40cm* *2017*

CAIAPHAS

It is easy to shout things down
To say that everything and everyone is wrong.
So many look upon my efforts with a sneer
As they drunkenly sing rebellion songs.
Easy for them to dream of a revolution
That would see us crushed into the dirt.
I take the harder road and compromise
With Roman officers, no matter that it hurts
My dignity and everything that I believe is right.
For if I did not trade in Roman coin and word
Who would soften the talons of the eagle?
Who would stop the swinging of the Roman sword?
There is no end of prophets in this land
Like the carpenter, who would lead us all to hang on trees,
But there are far too few who understand
That the survival of our race depends on pragmatists like me.

HERMIT SONG

In the beginning was the word
That poured like music from your lips
Into our very bones and all we were
Until they silenced up your mouth with death
But I had swallowed the fire of your blood
And ran half mad with longing
Out into the world
Spreading your words like
Paint doused into a water jar
Altering substance beyond return
Like wind, I sent your story out
Never silent - my words in short staccato bursts
As youth ran out -
Because I knew
That time was not my friend
Until, like muscle,
Certainty began to melt away

I looked around then at the ones I had inspired
Driven wild by the very fire I took from you
Or was it?
Was I sure?
Their concrete truth an unbending thing
I could no longer recognise as mine.
And so my words dried up
One by one until
I was left with the final comfort of silence
And the sea
And the wind
And regret
And isolation
As I pine
For death
For truth
For you

HERMIT SONG
Oil on Canvas
40cm x 40cm 2016

DESERT

What else is there for me to do
When I am vast and fierce and cannot be contained
But look on at man,
No more significant to me
Than the snake the twists across my skin
Or the beetles struggling to roll dung
Or the little wisps of scrub insisting they will stay
No matter what my mood?

Why should I be concerned
When I have seen a million, million men
Throughout my time,
Each struggling to set his mark
Upon my ever changing face?
Nothing human stands for very long.
In my savage, quiet and ageless world
All monuments to vanity must fall.

Why then would I note in a special way
The soft slap of a carpenter's feet
Those times he passed through my relentless sands?
But for some time since he came
Others have been happy to spill
And sacrifice their blood across
My parched and greedy gut.
Perhaps I should have noted him –
Or perhaps not.

DESERT

Oil on Canvas
60cm x 50cm 2015

Brenda Fitzmaurice

Brenda lives and works in Moyvane, Co. Kerry. Brenda is married to the poet and writer Gabriel Fitzmaurice. They have two children. She has worked for many years as an artist and an illustrator.

Brenda works predominantly with oils and palate knives but she always has a sketchbook and pencils in her bag.

Her work has largely been inspired by the ancient landscape of North Kerry.

She exhibits as a solo artist and in group exhibitions.

BF

Mary Kennelly

Mary Kennelly is married with three children and lives with her family in Glin, Co Limerick. She spent many years working in Special Education and is now Principal of Coláiste na Trócaire Secondary School. She is also a published poet and writer and has worked in the arts for many years.

Creative Writing

Editor – Winners Anthology Writer's Week 1996, 1997, 1998 & 1999
Editor – Brendan Kennelly Summer Festival Inaugural Souvenir Booklet 2000
'Sunny Spells, Scattered Showers' Carroll R. & Kennelly M. Glenwood Press 2004 & 2005
'From the Stones' Fitzmaurice B. & Kennelly M. Evensong Publications 2010
'Catching Bats Takes Patience'   Kennelly M. Liberties Press 2015

Whitehouse Poetry Anthology 2012 – Contributor

'Where I find God' – Contributor Eds. Cora Guinnane & Joanne O'Brien Columba Press 2016

By agreement with the poet and publisher her poetry has appeared in various magazines and publications. Her poetry is also on display in Limerick Regional Hospital, St. Camillus' Hospital, the Bon Secours Hospital Cork & Milford Hospice, the Malton Hotel, Killarney and the Listowel Arms Hotel.

She has written on writers, poetry and the arts for newspapers including 'The Kerryman', 'The Sunday Tribune' and 'The Sunday Independent'.

Media & performance

The poet has been interviewed for 'The Kerryman', 'The Limerick Leader', 'The Sunday Tribune' and 'The Sunday Independent', 'The Examiner', Kerry Radio, Limerick 95 FM & RTE Radio 1 & Headstuff.org amongst others.

She has read at venues including Writers' Week Listowel, Ó Bhéal, The Whitehouse & 'The Spoken Word Stage' Electric Picnic.

She has delivered a lectures on 'The North Kerry Writers: John B. Keane, Bryan MacMahon, Maurice Walsh, Seán McCarthy and Brendan Kennelly' and 'The Kennelly Poets; Brendan, Paddy & Mary' for Skidmore University and for the Smithsonian Institute as part of their credited outreach courses.

'Lament for a Lost Child' Tuesday Poem - The Examiner 01.09.2015

Links:

http://t.co/ul4C4PUMgf

http://media.radiokerry.ie/mediamanager/embed/player/podcasts/32/item/40535

PRINTS, POEMS & PAINTINGS

Prints are available of any of the poems and paintings in the book through Evensong Publications.

Enquiries about any of the original paintings to Evensong Publications.

CONTACT US

 evensongpublications@gmail.com

facebook.com/evensongpublications

 HUNGER PAINS   *Oil on Canvas   40cm x 40cm   2015*   BF

HUNGER PAINS

No chores today - we left early,
Wrapped against the morning breeze.
My mother and father smiling,
Swinging me as they walked.
Out from our village and up and up
Until we were surrounded by others -
So many others - travelling as well.
All day we listened to words
Passed along by the crowds.
As my father heard he called them out
Again and again and again

As he looked into my mother's eyes.
They did not notice the day go by
But I did for I was hungry.
I began, after a time, to cry
Big tears filled with my tragedy.
Then there was food -
Bread and fish -
I ate away at my will.
And I felt everything was right,
I was once again happy
As we walked home in dark.